TRIGGERED

TRIGGERED

Enjoli Gibbs

Some names and identifying details have been changed to protect the privacy of individuals.

Published in the United States by Enjoli Gibbs.

TRIGGERED. Copyright © 2020 by Enjoli Gibbs.

All rights reserved. No part of this book may be reproduced or transmitted in any form or by any means, electronic or mechanical, without prior written consent of the publisher, except for the inclusion of brief quotes in a review.

Printed in the United States of America. For information, city and state Cincinnati, Oh 45213.

ISBN: 9781734973204

Library of Congress Control Number: 2020907668

ACKNOWLEDGMENTS

First and foremost, I wanted to thank my Heavenly Father for allowing me to have the opportunity to share my journey.

Husband, you are amazing. Your love, support, patience, and consistency has truly showed me the evidence of God's love here on Earth. Thank you for continuing to push me to greatness.

Mom and Dad, thank you for continuing to support me in anyway you can. I can never repay you for the sacrifices made. But I sure will try.

Arlinda, thank you being a friend. Traveled down a road and back again. Your heart is true, you're a friend and a confidant. Before you ask, yes, I just quoted a lyric from the Golden Girls theme song. It's fitting. Thank you for not only being a friend, but for unselfishly guiding me through the process of self-publishing.

I have to give a shout out to my day one's Danielle Partridge and Crystal Shotwell. We've have been down since UC choir days 16 years ago. Quiera, Lauren, Curtrese, Natalie, T'wanda, thank y'all for the most hilariously entertaining supportive friendship ever. You all know I am not one to express a whole lot of emotions and be all sappy. But I love you all dearly.

Prologue

This book doesn't end with my Prince Charming. It begins with going back to my Heavenly Father.

Get ready for an emotional rollercoaster ride. It was 2012 and I was 24 years old, cute, and *miserable*. I'm not really the complaining type, but my life at the time sucked. For whatever reason, I just couldn't keep my head above water. I was so sick and tired of being hurt, especially by those who claimed to love me. I was tired of trying. I was tired of trying *and* getting knocked several steps backwards every time I did try. No matter what I did, I failed *miserably*.

I had my child when I was 19 years old, as I was entering my sophomore year in college. I got *bamboozled*! *Hoodwinked*! This fool sold me a *whole* dream. It wasn't funny then, but I chuckle about it now. I completely fell for the okie doke. Hell, that's part of why I'm in this mess now. He isn't around, except for occasional showboating on holidays.

The holiday-only involvement really burned my biscuits. How could you do that to a child? A child deserves more than just a few phone calls a year and sporadic visits. No parent should have to carry the load of parenting by themselves. There I was, with no family, trying to take care of this child the best way I could. In a word, I was *tired*.

People only "love" you as long as they can get something from you. As soon as you say, "No," or decide you want better than the scraps they're giving you, they hit you with the middle finger emoji.

If you looked in the table of contents, you saw all the different characters or phases. I'm not crazy. But these characters or phases I experienced were interesting, to say the least. They were triggered by past experiences in my life a *long*, *long* time ago, probably as far back as childhood. I didn't notice them until my earlier twenties, when it seemed like my life had started to plummet. The hurt and emotions I felt drove me nuts. I had to get a hold on things.

I "gave in" to these characters. I took their advice. They seemed to care. They told me how I needed to think and feel about different things. They altered how I perceived things. It was easier. Sure, I could try to address my deeply rooted issues and not let these characters determine the compass for my life. But who was trying to do all that work? I didn't have that type of time.

So, I thought.

Prideful Patty
3/15/2012

Prideful Patty is the one person who caused the most trouble in my life. I've lost a lot. I didn't want to trust people. I'd been hurt too many times by the people the closest to me. Even though I was in deep trouble, I didn't want to ask for help because people would throw it up in my face later. People will hold you hostage. They're going to want something more. They really don't want to help you. They want to use you.

I believed I should hide my hurt because no one really cared genuinely anyway. I'd get over it eventually. I didn't need anyone! I also thought I was experiencing depression or anxiety, but I couldn't say that out loud. You know, "Black people don't deal with mental illness. They are gonna say you're crazy, girl!"

I was working for a company where I wore many hats. I was a field worker, personal assistant, and administrator. It was a *tad* overwhelming, to say the least. But I handled it well. I could handle the overwhelming part. My life was already a tangled web of depression and overwhelm. But I was stretched so thin. There weren't any boundaries. My job duties went past the normal work hours of 8 a.m. to 5 p.m. Things got so bad that I almost lost my job.

My boss looked at me, as I stared emotionlessly back at him, and said, "You need some help. Like some serious help."

I *did*. I was battling depression and anxiety so badly that I went numb. At that time, I was losing in life. *Badly.* I was in the process of being evicted and trying to find a place to live for me and the kid. I was dealing with a hostile environment at work. The place where I found value in being overworked was the very place that was throwing me away. The reason I was in the situation in the first place is because the same person who told me I needed help (my boss) was the same person who was cutting my hours whenever he felt like it. It seemed like whenever I created boundaries, things went downhill. The same person fired me three days later when I put in a three-week notice. I already wasn't being compensated what I was worth. But, when people don't have a hold on you anymore, if they can't manipulate or play on your loyalty, it's a problem. I lost my place to live. I was already in the process of leaving; it just wasn't happening fast enough.

All my family was in Cleveland. My mom knew something was going on, but I didn't tell her. No one knew the real deal. All I knew was I had to shield my daughter from what was happening. All she knew was that we were moving to a new place (which I hadn't found yet) that wasn't ready. The icing on the cake was that Friday, I had to be out of my place. I still had to work at the place that played with my money and helped cause my eviction. On my lunch break, I called some shelters. Oddly enough, the shelters wouldn't let me come because, *technically*, I still had a residence. I had to wait until Monday to call.

At that point, I figured we would have to sleep in my car. I found an apartment that was nice enough to rent to me, despite my circumstances. However, it wouldn't be ready for another three weeks. I had a couple of friends. But after being mistreated and betrayed, I didn't trust anyone. I simply told my daughter that we were "camping out." We would sleep in my Impala until I could figure things out. All I had to do was manage for three weeks. My mom would get my daughter for at least a week since it was summertime. I had it all planned out.

My plan worked. I managed to shield my daughter from the craziness. I told my daughter we were going camping. In her mind, we were moving and simply had to wait for our place to be ready. As the days passed, I honestly didn't know if I was coming or going. I moved. But I only had enough for a small storage space, which was enough for my loveseat, clothes, and a few other items. I lost our beds and any other big items.

One thing I am grateful for is that, during that three-week period, a wonderful person opened their doors to me. We were in a small one-bedroom apartment, on an air mattress, in the living room. We lived out of bags. It could have been worse. She didn't have to let us in, but she did.

In addition to all of this, I was talking to a sorry excuse of a man who only cared about himself. His outlook on life was twisted. I told him about what was going on in my life and explained that I couldn't see him anymore. I had too many things going on and I needed to focus. But we could still be cool though.

This fool said, "I understand you have priorities and things you have to handle. I just thought I was one of them."

I thought to myself, *No this fool didn't!* He didn't say, "I understand" or "Let me know if you need anything." At this point, I felt nothing. I couldn't take "feeling" anything else. I was literally a shell of a person, walking around functioning in my dysfunction.

I dug myself into a bigger hole because I didn't ask for help. I still needed help! Yet, after being mistreated in the manner in which I was, I couldn't bring myself to ask anyone for anything. People already looked down on me. They treated me like yesterday's trash. Pride hurt me. It blinded me. I could've asked someone for help. I could've asked God to lead me to the *right* people or resources. But I didn't.

Reflection

Do you find yourself being a Prideful Patty? Circle: YES or NO. Why?

_____

_____

_____

_____

_____

_____

_____

_____

_____

_____

Everything has a root. What triggers your pride? When did this start?

Notes

Affirmations to Overcome

It's not easy to get past being prideful. But it's doable.

It's a lifelong journey.

When you are in a situation and feel your pride rising,

speak these affirmations out loud:

Vulnerability *does not* equal weakness.

Asking for help *does not* make you incompetent.

Being soft doesn't mean you are a *punk*.

It takes courage and strength to admit and ask for help.

You are *strong* and *courageous*.

You are *more* than enough.

You are *fearfully* and *wonderfully* made

(Psalm 139:14).

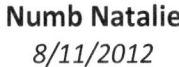

Numb Natalie
8/11/2012

After what I went through with that fool, I went into my "numb" place. I can't explain the anguish and hurt I felt. Being thrown away like yesterday's trash, dismissed like I was nothing, made me feel like I had no one. These people sucked the life out of me. Then, they kicked me to the curb once I had nothing left to give *or* once I decided not to give anymore. Let me throw this in there. I'm a PK (preacher's kid) and church girl. I never left the church. I was up in there every Sunday, just as broken as they come. But that's another story for another book.

All I knew was, at that moment, I couldn't bear to "feel" anymore. So, I buried it. Every bit of hurt, pain, disappointment, and brokenness, I put it up. I was ice cold from that day forward. My numb place is my safe place. Well, at least that's what I thought.

I didn't realize that, although I'd "put away" my brokenness, it still seeped out. I thought I was still empathetic toward people (even though I wasn't toward myself). Apparently, I was wrong. People thought I was a bit rough around the edges. I was kind of mean or standoffish. Perhaps subconsciously, I treated people the way I was treated. I concluded, at a young age, that people didn't care about my feelings. I was in so much pain as a child. For a moment in time, I started cutting myself with a box cutter. I cut in areas that weren't noticeable, at first. But, one day, I cut a mural into my left arm. There were a couple of birds, a sun, a hump for a grassy area, and a flower. I think I had a couple of clouds, too. I don't know how long I had it before someone noticed it at a Sunday afternoon musical. The pastor of the church we were visiting noticed and asked why I did it.

I said, "I don't know."

His response was, "Well, don't do it again." We were in a *whole church* and the *pastor* didn't bother to pray for me! Maybe he didn't do anything because I was his pastor friend's daughter. After all, we couldn't have the pastor's kids looking crazy. Maybe he didn't want to make anyone "look bad." He did tell my parents about it, though.

They weren't sad. They didn't yell. They didn't take me to therapy, and they didn't even pray for me. They simply told me not to do it anymore. In that very moment, it dawned on me that *not even my own parents* offered to pray with me. I'd witnessed my parents praying for others on a *weekly* basis. I saw them offer so much compassion for people. I got the short end of the compassion stick, though.

Maybe I needed attention. I stopped cutting myself shortly after that. That day was the day I realized *no one* cared about my feelings.

I know I should probably be praying and giving my hurt to God. But what good is that, honestly? I'm the person everyone else tells their hurts and pains to when they're going through it. That's my God-given purpose. No one cares about my feelings. That's been proven time and time again. If you're numb, you won't feel anything. Right? No more hurt, right? Problem solved!

Reflection

Do you find yourself being a Numb Natalie? Circle: YES or NO. Why?

Everything has a root. What triggers your numb state?

When did this start?

Affirmations to Overcome

It's not easy to get past being numb. But it's doable.

It's a lifelong journey.

When you are in a situation and you feel yourself

slipping into your numb place,

speak these affirmations out loud:

It is okay to feel.

It is *necessary* to face yourself and the pain.

It is *okay* to not be *okay* sometimes.

You can put the cape away and *rest*.

You are *strong* and *courageous*.

You are *more* than enough.

You are *fearfully* and *wonderfully* made

(Psalm 139:14).

Helpful Hattie
9/21/2012

That's me. You got a problem? I can help you! I'm your girl! Let me grab my cape. I finally found the solution (so I thought). I got more involved in church. Even when it was too much, it was okay. There's a sense of fulfillment in helping others. God's happy, right? It's funny—during this stage, I heard things like, "Indulge in self-care." I don't even know what that is for real. I had consistent "occasional" breakdowns in private. But that's only because I lost focus, not because all I was doing was piling up broken pieces and it was spilling over. I can't stand *myself* sometimes.

Where on earth did I get that foolishness from? Clearly, there was something going on in my heart. Who has breakdowns "consistently occasionally" and is actually okay? I used being "helpful" as my Band-Aid. I didn't get the attention I needed when I cut myself. However, I received praise and recognition from parents when I helped with whatever they needed. I received the same praise and recognition from the other adults, too. I finally figured it out. That's what I needed.

That behavior carried on into adulthood. It was a very unhealthy behavioral trait. How did I become an overlooked overachiever? Even though I tried to be the ideal model child, it just turned into an expectation.

"Oh, we know she's going to be good. She's always going to help. She'll get it together," other people always said. Soon enough, the recognition I sought and thought I'd found turned into what I was *supposed* to do. I couldn't win for losing.

I learned to live without love. I told myself that I didn't need it. The truth is that most people desire love and affection, regardless of if it is platonic or romantic. It's in the basic hierarchy of our needs. I told myself that I didn't need people to care about me, although I wanted them to. I used to imagine something tragic happening to me. If

something happened to me, people would care for once. It would be so nice to have people care.

This is where the "ah-ha" moment came to me. I couldn't figure out, for the life of me, why the men I chose to date were not that great. Now, don't get me wrong. Most of them were decent human beings. But they always seemed to have deep wounds or internal issues. I could help them. I could "love" them through their trauma. I know, I know! How could I possibly love them when I clearly didn't love myself? I could help manifest their potential. They needed *my* help. But that's not a romantic relationship. Was I a significant other or a case worker? On top of all that, I lived a life, believing I didn't need love to be reciprocated.

That was an ugly cycle that I created for myself. *Help.* Everyone needed help. I needed to *help* people because "that's what I do." Or was it because, deep down, I was looking for something? Love? Not romantic love, but for people to care about me in the same manner I did for them?

Reflection

Do you find yourself being a Helpful Hattie? Circle: YES or NO. Why?

_____

_____

_____

_____

_____

_____

_____

_____

_____

_____

Everything has a root. What triggers your helpfulness? Is it sincere, or is it a cover-up for a deeper issue?

Affirmations to Overcome

It's not easy to get past being unnecessarily helpful.

But it's doable. It's a lifelong journey.

When you are in a situation and you feel yourself

taking on too much, speak these affirmations out loud:

It is *okay* to say, "No!"

Not everyone is your assignment, e

ven if it is a close friend or family member.

It is crucial to have healthy boundaries with people.

It is okay to change your mind.

You are *strong* and *courageous*.

You are *more* than enough.

You are *fearfully* and *wonderfully* made

(Psalm 139:14).

Bitter Betty
5/8/2013

Let's be clear: I was a *whole* mess. *A whole mess.* When I was in my 20s, my life was an entire mess. I didn't realize how bitter I was until after the fact. I constantly compared myself to others. It seemed like everyone around me was doing so much better in life than me. It appeared like they had accomplished everything I was supposed to accomplish. Everything that I dreamed about and desired seemed to happen to, and for, everyone else. I watched my peers graduate from college. I, on the other hand, had to drop out to take care of my child. Everyone around me had quality jobs. I could barely make ends meet. I wanted a healthy, meaningful relationship. But all I received was an offer for friends with benefits or situation-ships. Everyone else around me found "the one." They were getting engaged and married. I had a saying at the time: "These hoes are winning." Trust me, they were. I was holding out and getting nothing but heartache.

    I can't explain how hard that made my heart. I was so upset that I was left tarnished. I have a child whom I am the sole provider for, with minimal help from her father or that side of her family altogether. He got to move on and live his life while he left mine shattered in millions of pieces. Of course, I didn't want him back. But it was so disheartening to see him have the option to move on while I lived in misery. It wasn't fair! He was the one who did me dirty and dogged me. But he was the one who received the rewards of life while I was left in the trenches. I was left in the trenches, and every person I was there for left me there, too. They got what they needed and left me high and dry.

I gave too many people too much power over my life. I gave them too much say so. I let people manipulate my situation to the point I had my own mini Job experience. It's one thing to play with my mind or my heart. It's another thing to play with my emotions. But when you play with my money, it's a whole other situation. *Never* be in a situation where someone can have control over you and your paycheck. That was a hard lesson I had to learn.

I told myself, "Eff all of them! You ain't gonna forgive them. They don't deserve that. Look at you. Look at your situation. Look at how bad you're struggling. You've lost jobs, lost a place to live and lost cars. You were partially homeless for a few weeks. Your lights have been cut off. You lost the food in your fridge. It's all *their* fault and everyone else who has taken advantage of you. I know the Bible teaches you to forgive as God forgave you. But, why? That ain't helping you. Look around, man! Everyone is receiving all of *your* desires. God ain't thinking about you. He forgot about you. You might as well just be satisfied with being nothing more than just someone men want to sleep with, or a person who people want to take advantage of, use up all your talents and gifts. Or, you can be alone."

Reflection

Do you find yourself being a Bitter Betty? Circle: YES or NO. Why?

_____
_____
_____
_____
_____
_____
_____
_____
_____
_____

Everything has a root. What triggers your bitterness?

Affirmations to Overcome

It's not easy to get past bitterness. But it's doable.

It's a lifelong journey.

When you are in a situation and you feel your heart hardening,

speak these affirmations out loud:

It is okay to forgive,

even if I *never* receive acknowledgment or an apology.

Forgiveness is for *me*, not the other person.

I can and I *will* let go of any emotional

baggage attached to an offense so

I can be *free* and *happy*.

You are *strong* and *courageous*.

You are *more* than enough.

You are *fearfully* and *wonderfully* made

(Psalm 139:14).

Mean Martha
7/19/2014

To be honest, I didn't know I was "mean" at all. Was I a *teeny* bit bitter on the inside? Perhaps. I've heard I can be a little abrasive. At the time, my thought process was, "No one cares about my feelings, so I have to toughen up. No one cares." I'd give it to you straight, no chaser. It may have hurt, but it was the truth. No one had a problem telling me the truth about me. No one had a problem telling me whatever twisted version of the truth they thought. (It wasn't God's truth.) No one cared or even bothered to ask if I was okay. They didn't bother to see past my "seemingly okay" exterior to the darkness inside of me. I just treated people how people treated me.

Even when I did show an inkling of hurt or displeasure, I'd get the, "Well, you'll get over it" response. Others told me, "Suck it up. You'll be all right." People always had something to say to me, but no one ever asked if I was okay. I was the overlooked overachiever. I was the bitter, numb lady who wanted nothing more than for someone just to care. People thought I was mean. I am sweet as pie on the inside. No one ever really knew the real, authentic me for a long time.

Mean Martha told me, "If I were you, I'd stick to being Mean Martha. These people don't care about you. Honestly sis, you need to make sure you get them before they get you! Everybody is out to hurt you anyway. You can't let no one—absolutely no one—in. The only 'person' you need is yourself. You've made it this far without having close relationships, right? You may have had a lot of issues, but *you* have been the only one to stick around. Everyone else left you hanging."

Reflection

Do you find yourself being a Mean Martha? Circle: YES or NO. Why?

_____

_____

_____

_____

_____

_____

_____

_____

_____

_____

Everything has a root. What triggers your meanness?

Affirmations to Overcome

It's not easy to get past being mean. But it's doable.

It's a lifelong journey.

When you are in a situation

and you feel yourself wanting to be unkind,

speak these affirmations out loud:

You are *not* defined by your defense mechanisms.

You can be strong without being *hard*.

It takes more strength to be kind to others,

even if it is not reciprocated.

You are *strong* and *courageous*.

You are *more* than enough.

You are *fearfully* and *wonderfully* made

(Psalm 139:14).

Worthless Wendy
10/31/2015

Somewhere in this roller coaster of a mess called my emotions, even though I didn't utter the words, I felt worthless. I wasn't good enough. I felt like I was always in last place. Life would be no more than what it was now. No one would ever love me. Failed attempt after failed attempt. I wanted more in life. I wanted to stop the hurt that would burst from my heart out of nowhere. I wanted to be free. The weight of the world was so heavy at times. I felt weighed downed physically. I knew I was depressed. My world was filled with so much sorrow. I had no zeal for life. During all of that, I still had to hold all my broken pieces together for my daughter. Life had shattered my self-esteem, self-worth, self-image, and my entire outlook on life. I hated to look at myself in the mirror. All I saw were my flaws—everything that was wrong with me.

So many times, I wanted to end it all. I convinced myself that my child was better off without me. I wrapped a cord around my throat. The plan was to wrap the other end on my ceiling fan while it was going. I had everything written down on how I wanted things to go with my child. No one would be affected by my nonexistence. To them, I was no one. I gave everyone everything that I had to give—spiritually, emotionally, physically, and monetarily. There was no more praise. No more fulfillment in helping others.

Everyone took what they could get until they couldn't anymore. My mind was in a fog. A million incomplete thoughts spiraled out of control in my shell of a mind. Everything around me was moving in slow motion. I couldn't even cry anymore.

However, no one knew that I felt worthless. What would be the point of telling someone how I felt? From a young age, doing that had failed me every time. When I tried to express how I felt, my feelings were minimized or ignored. Sometimes, the person who was supposed to be listening would "relate" to what I was feeling and, somehow, the conversation turned around to be about *them*. I wasn't gonna let anybody catch me slipping. Me and my daughter were cute. I put my makeup on every day! I kept my hair cute. I made sure I coordinated. When my lights were off, you would never know. My makeup was still tight, even if I had to put it on in the dark. I figured I'd fake it 'til I made it! I stayed stocked with waterproof mascara. No one would ever know the tears I cried.

Reflection

Do you find yourself being a Worthless Wendy? Circle: YES or NO. Why?

_____

_____

_____

_____

_____

_____

_____

_____

_____

Everything has a root. What triggers your feelings of worthlessness?

___

___

___

___

___

___

___

___

___

___

___

Affirmations to Overcome

It's not easy to get past feelings of despair. But it's doable.

It's a lifelong journey.

When you are in a situation and you feel low,

speak these affirmations out loud:

You are *amazing*.

You are *remarkable*.

You are *valuable*.

You are *strong* and *courageous*.

You are *more* than enough.

You are *fearfully* and *wonderfully* made

(Psalm 139:14).

Accountability

At this point, I'd had enough. I was tired of fighting, struggling, surviving, and barely making it. I couldn't take being depressed or the heartache, fatigue, and the crying. Everyone around me was so happy and full of life. I decided that I wanted that, too. I wanted to live life to the fullest. I wanted to be healed. I wanted to be free from every emotional bondage that I'd tangled myself up in over the years.

The process of healing was a gruesome one. Of course, the first step was admitting that I had some—a lot—of issues. That was easy. The next part for me is what had me in a tizzy. I had to take accountability for the part I'd played in my hurt. Yes, you heard me correctly. No one can do more to you than you allow them to. (NOTE: I am not talking about extreme situations with physical abuse where your life is threatened.) I'm talking about those situations where you allowed someone to hurt you over and over. You accepted less than God's best for you but got mad at Him like He did something wrong. God didn't have anything to do with my bad decisions. In fact, the more I thought about it, there were *several* red flags that I ignored. I ignored my discernment or intuition when it came to people. I second-guessed myself. I got burned every time.

As if that wasn't hard enough, the next step I took was backtracking. I had to trace where these behaviors came from. Everything always has a root, a starting place. I had to trace the root of why I chose the men I chose to date. I had to trace the root of why I let people use me and take advantage of me. I had to trace the root of why I wanted to help so much yet didn't accept help. Each question led to a path of discovery. Sometimes, it was long. It hurt to go backwards. I'm glad I did, though. It showed me my reference point of why I did the things that I did. From that reference point, a behavior was created, whether good or bad. A perception is created that dictates how you operate and function. I found where it stemmed from and made the effort to replace that reference point with something different. It changed my behavior and perception of things.

Reference Points

We all have a "reason" why we think, act, and perceive things the way we do. We watch our parents, family, or friends. We experience a variety of things in life, good and bad. Depending on the outcome of these experiences, that determines the reference point or behavior that is formed from that point forward. For instance, in earlier stages in life, I concluded that no one cared about me and that I didn't need love. It stemmed from the event of a need not being met. Making that conclusion created a bad habit and a bad perception. That created a cycle of dysfunction.

This dysfunction affected multiple areas of my life. Often, we think that trauma affects one area that's related to the circumstance. Not true. I made poor dating choices because of this conclusion. I didn't receive reciprocation of the love I gave because I didn't "need" it. I entertained people who didn't have my best interest at heart. This didn't just apply to romantic relationships. It played a part in my platonic relationships as well. It didn't matter if they were male or female. Some friendships turned out to be the same sort of scenario. They "needed" me. It was typically one-sided. I only needed to be *needed* by people. That's where I found a sense of fulfillment. It was only a temporary fix, though. A trail of tears and heartbreak came from those experiences. I couldn't break that cycle unless I knew where it came from. That's why I had to backtrack.

It wasn't enough to just find the reference point. I had to create a better habit to replace the bad one. For instance, I had to stop feeding people that only wanted a "to-go" plate. They didn't buy any grocery, plate, or cutlery, or even contribute a juice box. But they always had Tupperware. I had to say, "No!" when necessary and be okay with it. I had to distance myself from people who did nothing but take from me. I had to create better relational habits for the right people who came along in my life. It's not enough just to get over the hurt. If you don't change your bad behavior, it will hurt the *right* people who are in your life.

I had to seek God to bring the right people into my life. Some people say, "When you know better, you do better." You learn better by doing something different and better. I had to get around people who had a different, better outlook on life. I wanted God-centered, reciprocal relationships. So, I had to get around people who reflected that to learn what "better" looked like. I read articles and books to develop a better outlook. It was trial and error from that point on. What worked for others didn't always work for me. But I was diligent enough to find what did work for me. Things got better *slowly*.

Forgiveness was a doozy, but necessary. It was easier to forgive those who had hurt, failed, used, and abused me after I took accountability. I no longer blamed them fully for my broken pieces. It helped me realize that forgiveness truly was for me. Having the ability to let go of the emotional response attached to the pain gave me the opportunity to let other things in, including God's love, peace, and healing.

The Kicker

Someone told me something that changed my life forever. She told me, "If I knew how much God really loved me, I wouldn't accept any type of treatment from *anyone*. I wouldn't accept any less than God's best." This *blew* my mind! I thought I knew God. I've been in church my whole life, even as an adult.

But being "in church" didn't mean that I had a relationship with God. I had habits that involved God. Is it possible that how I functioned in my relationships with people on earth is how I functioned in my relationship with God? If I did things that were pleasing in His sight, I was good, right? I tithed. I served. All of the above. If I did good, He was happy (Helpful Hattie). It's almost like being transactional with God versus relational. The disappointment came when I discovered that's just simply *not* how God works. You can't barter with Him. Nor can you treat Him like a genie in a bottle that you just come to when you want or need something.

Sometimes, it felt like God was so far away. It felt like even He had forgotten about me. I would ask Him for things, and He didn't give them to me. I didn't understand that, because I lived my life, trying to do the "right" thing, I needed help. Although my decision-making was the reason why I was in a bad place, I still needed Him to get me out. Transactional-ships don't work. I needed a relationship. I didn't know how to have a relationship with anyone. Period. I had to go back to the drawing board. Well, a relationship consists of at least two people. Both parties bring different things to the relationship, some similarities and some differences. Both parties give and take, and they find a healthy balance. You get to know each other. Both people give the same or necessary amount of attention the other person needs. They also listen as they need. You enjoy being around each other. They support you and, hopefully, they tell you right from wrong.

If these are the basics of a healthy relationship with someone (platonic or romantic), I *clearly* didn't have this with God. I went back to His Word, reading and studying what I thought I already knew. I learned about His promises, what He likes and dislikes. I started to talk to Him every day throughout the day. I wasn't asking Him for anything. I talked to Him like He was my friend.

Side Note: Doesn't it burn your biscuits when people only call or talk to you when they want something? They don't ask how you are or even know if you are okay. They haven't done *anything* for you lately. Yet, they have the audacity and gall to ask you for something. Imagine how God feels. Once I got to know Him on a different level, my life started to change. My perception changed. My behavior changed. My discernment sharpened. It was easier to see what true colors are when I met new people.

I even got to know myself better. As I healed, I found different things about me that were trapped up under all that hurt and pain. I found different talents, skills, and interests. There was so much to me. I discovered things that I enjoyed doing. I started to live, not just exist. I was able to genuinely smile each day when I'd cried for so many years. I found joy in seeing the sunshine or the sound of the rain during a thunderstorm. I finally learned how to be present. I focused so much on the next thing, needing this or that, that the years came and went, and life just passed me by.

My prayer for you is that, if you are how I used to be, you choose to break through any trauma or horrible experience that caused a never-ending cycle of hurt and bad decisions. Some things may have happened to you when you were just a child. It's not your fault. But it is your fault if you decide to live with the residue of trauma when you have a choice not to. It's not an easy road. The process never ends. It gets better when you put in the work. If you don't have a relationship with God, try it out. If you have one and lost your way, I encourage you to find your way back. Start with this book. If necessary, seek a counselor. It's okay. I promise you it is. Jesus + Therapy is a great recipe for healing and living an abundant life. Be blessed, girl!

An Invitation

If you didn't know, I want you to know that God loves you. He sent His son Jesus to die on the cross for all our sins so we may have the chance at eternal life. He gives us the opportunity of salvation, which is accepting Him as your Lord and Savior. Imagine being in relationship with someone like that. Someone that loves you unconditionally, even when you do wrong, despite your flaws. He gives us grace and mercy each day. The best part is His forgiveness! When you have a relationship with God and you sin, you have a chance to repent and go back to Him. You can ask for forgiveness. He forgets the sin in just that instant! If you're ready for change in your life, pray this prayer:

Father, I come to you, wanting to invite you into my life and to surrender my life to you. I believe you sent your Son to die for our sins and paid the ultimate price so I may have a chance at eternal life. I ask for forgiveness for my sins and that you create in me a clean heart. From this day forward, I accept you in my life as my Lord and Savior and ask that you fill me with the Holy Spirit. In Jesus' name! Amen!